Seriously Joking
The Unofficial Guide to
Happiness

Johnnie Busch Jr.

Dedication

I dedicate this book to everyone that has made an impact on my life. You have taught me how to live this life and truly live everyday with hope and peace. I thank everyone who has had an impact on my life.

Table of Contents

INTRODUCTION

Hello there! How are you? Thank you for purchasing this book. Hopefully you didn't steal it. However, if you did, I love you anyway. First and foremost, if no one has ever said it to you, I want to say "I love you". I love you because you are my brother and sister in Christ. One of the reasons I decided to write this book is because I thought I never could write it. This book has been on my mind for quite some time. As you read it, my prayer is that you find your inner peace. This book is not meant to be deep; it's not to bash any one person; and it is not a guideline for your life. This is simply my experience and the things I have learned along the way. As you read this book I hope you take the few things that you need and realize that you can live a better life. I was put on this earth to share many things, and as we go through this book you will get a better understanding of who I am. Let this book be whatever it needs to be for your life. This book is a small glimpse into my life. It is not a professional "how to." I share a few helpful nuggets. Don't expect a lengthy book but a short story that proves to help you live a long, happy and healthy life. I must write a disclaimer, however. For all the religious people out there this book may not be for you. The book is not vulgar but I reveal things that some people may not agree with. I say religious because we are taught to have a religion and not a relationship with God. I'm all about being free. A lot of religious people are quick to judge others and forget so quickly where they came from. The opinions and facts in this book are solely based on my life; no animals were harmed in the making of this book. Alright, now that I got that out the way. LET'S HAVE A GOOD TIME!

Chapter 1
Who is Johnnie Busch?

*Romans 12:2 Do not be conformed to this world
but be transformed by the renewal of your mind,
that by testing you may discern what is the will of
God, what is good and acceptable and perfect.*

Who is Johnnie Busch? Well, sit back and relax because I'm getting ready to tell you. I, Johnnie Busch was born on May 22, 1990 in Atlanta, Georgia. I am the birth son of Johnnie Busch Sr. and Peggy Ann Busch. I have 7 sisters and no brothers. I'm not spoiled! I won't go through all of my childhood events but I will talk about some particular things that may spark your interest. I grew up in a town called College Park, Georgia and then I moved to Fayetteville, Georgia while in the 3rd grade. Moving from one city to the next helped me to adapt to people and events a lot quicker. I have been able to absolutely love the skin that I'm in without having any regrets. The confidence that I have acquired today came from my faith (which I will talk about later) and my parents.

I believe that parents are one of the most if not the most influential persons in your life. I could not answer the question "Who is Johnnie Busch?" without my parents. Sadly, my mother passed away the day after my third birthday, on Sunday May 23, 1993. My mother reportedly passed after a long battle with breast cancer. I'm asked all the time, how does it feel to grow up without a mother? I must admit that it was and still is at times, a tough pill to swallow. My dad has always been in my life. I will acknowledge him later in the chapter. Because I was so young, I never knew my mother. I can't believe I'm saying this... "I NEVER KNEW MY MOTHER!"

Life has an interesting way of unfolding. I often think about where my life would be with my mother. Would I live where I live now? Would I still have a love for theatre? Would I even be writing this book? There are many more questions to ask. However, in my opinion the biggest question may be, "what has that experience taught you"? The experience of not having your biological mother is a storyline like no other.

I'm grateful for VHS tapes because that is how I knew my mother. I'm told that she was such a clean freak that she put her dish rags in the refrigerator so that bugs won't fly on the dish rags. I've gotten to experience her walk, her laugh and her entire demeanor through video. As I look at my life I see myself in her in many ways; But I put food in the refrigerator not my dish rags.

(Smiles)

She was honest, God fearing, loving, and a mother who loved all three of her children with all of her heart. This book is dedicated to an angel and my mother from heaven, Ms. Peggy Ann Busch. She is looking down laughing at the crazy things I do, frowning when I'm unpleasant and smiling when I serve others. Momma (tears) I love you and I will see you soon.

I can't talk about women that have influenced my life and not talk about my step mother Marsha Busch. She is a loving mother and God placed her in my life for a period of time when I needed her the most. Being a step mother is a tough role and I want to show my appreciation to her for all of her sacrifices. Children always want their parents to stay together but what we want and God's plans are two different things.

I remember to this day when my dad and step mother sat my sisters and I down with the sad news. It was a weekday evening and everyone was in their bedroom. We were all called out to the dining room table to listen to some very important news. The facial expressions of my parents were not favorable. We were never called into one spot at an awkward time. I believe my dad started the conversation off with how they loved us and how time has moved on.

After about a quick five minutes, the news was broken that they were getting a divorce. They made it very clear that it was not us. I glanced around the table and everybody's face was dry. There was not a word spoken. After a few seconds one of my sisters' said "Why?" As natural as that question was, I don't believe it was clearly answered. It's one of those things that is really hard to talk about.

They exemplified how a husband and wife should act. They were a great team together. Life goes on and it gets sweeter. It was hard for everyone to talk for months and years later because we just didn't know which way to go. To my step mother, I thank you and I love you. You have done so much for my life and you handled your life with grace. I cherish your love!

My dad has been my right hand man since day one. Let's talk about who my dad is first because that will help you understand his impact on my life. My father is a Vietnam Veteran. He was hit by a grenade in the war. He is totally blind in both eyes. Every year he lost more and more sight. My dad has taught me more without sight than someone with sight. There is so much I can say about my father. He has been with me through boy scouts and with me in my swimming classes, (By the way I still can't swim). He has been to every theatre production. He has always cheered me on. Naturally my dad and I have disagreed and have argued many times. There are times where I hated him, loved him, feared him, was mad at him and then loved him again. The older I got the more I realized that a parent's love will always be there.

My dad has taught me a lot about commitment. He has once hosted a weekly radio program. I saw his commitment and love of God through the station every week. Callers could call in and give their testimonies and he would pray prayers that could raise the dead. God's word has always been in our house. I grew up in church and was heavily involved in the many different church programs. I embraced all of these stories in my life because I would not know who I am today without all these experiences.

I often say to people don't fight what comes naturally and don't apologize for how you feel because at one point you had that feeling. Don't deny yourself of what you feel you need.

God has a way of making your life come full circle. Everything that is happening in your life is needed for your growth. Have you ever tried to eat a cake and it was only half done?

God needs you to bring forth his plan. It will become very tiring when you try to fight what God is trying to do in your life. Your life is simply your life. The way you operate your life is the way that you have learned. How dare we take away someone's experience? I'm not trying to preach but I will add my mailing address for you to send me an offering as God leads your heart.

Who is Johnnie Busch? I'm a man of God. Ask yourself that same question. Don't answer the question until you are sure of your answer!

Chapter 2
The Principal's Office
was my Classroom

1 Corinthians 13:11 When I was a child, I spoke as a child, I understood as a child, I thought as a child; but when I became a man I put away childish things.

(Yelling) Johnnie, Johnnie, Johnnie, Johnnie, Johnnie!

Oh!" "Sorry I am here." That was how many times my teachers had to call my name. The principal's office was truly my classroom. I don't like the term class clown so I will just say that I was one the funniest kids in the school. I was an interesting character beginning with head start (pre school program) from high school all the way until I graduated. The interesting thing about comedy is that some things can't be planned or thought of, some of the best comedy acts are those that are acted upon on the spot.

The comedy in the classroom all started with my name. From the past to the present, I have not met one person who does not call me by either my first and last name together or just my last name. Classmates have said that my name is catchy. I never felt my name was catchy or popular, but obviously that's how others feel. The popularity of my name came much later. I knew I had talent to make people laugh or at the very least create something. When God gives you a talent, you have to use it before he takes it away. You maybe saying "Johnnie, the classroom is the last place to display your talent." I beg to differ.

I realized my talent was much bigger than I had ever imagined or dreamed of. You know you have a special gift when your own teachers laugh at what you say. I personally had one of my teacher's say, "it was so hard not to laugh." That moment right there is when I knew I had a gift. Each year I slowly unwrapped that gift and that became my first stage play which I will talk about later on. Don't underestimate a child's vision or dream because that dream can put you in a place where you belong.

Elementary school years were not the best

years for me because I was often picked on. I wore the same green jacket every day, not only did I wear the jacket everyday but I wore it all day. It may have provided me a source of comfort. Kids can find comfort in anything. I learned to stick up for myself and stand up to the bullies. I want to stop and thank everyone in elementary school that picked on me because I am now able to pay a lot more bills because of you. Thank you cards will be in the mail shortly. My elementary school teachers were more tolerable of behaviors than any other school grade. The older I've gotten I realized how harsh the teachers were. Elementary school was a place that I was still trying to figure out what I was doing, where I was and who I was. We sometimes don't want to go through the Genesis of life, but the beginning is where you find out all about who you are.

Middle school is where I really explored my talent outside of the classroom. I was a part of many talent shows. The first one that I remember was when a few friends and I lip synced, "My Girl" by The Temptations. I was really nervous and thought we couldn't pull it off. We were placed in a top spot and really had fun. Why should we go through life and not have any fun? If you are going to take this ride then, you should enjoy it. I was so excited to be a part of that event. I really was. I was even excited about recess. I think my teachers were more excited than I was because I let out all my energy on that day. I think most teachers were excited for recess too because they got a break from all the energy and clowning.

High school was much different than the other grade levels because we were more aware of the boundaries. For the average student, school is their classroom but for me school was my stage. When the morning bell rang that was my cue for the curtain to rise. I walked in that classroom and it was "ShowTime"! I looked forward to going to school each and every day. I didn't look forward to doing the work but I looked forward to meeting with my friends and enjoying fun filled day.

Elementary school gave me a real sense of childhood. I looked forward to recess every day.

My favorite playground activity was "The Swings." As soon as the bell rang, I would rush to the playground just to be the first person on the swing. It was something special that I enjoyed about going up higher and higher. It elevated my mind and I felt like a bird in the sky everyday around 12:30. I wasn't as popular in elementary school but things soon took a change.

Middle school was where I was slowly coming into myself. That's it, that's right, I was finding myself. Middle school was a place where I was in the principal's office literally almost every day. You would think going to the principal's office would be a scary thing, but going to the principal's office was almost always fun for me. That's right, most of the time I helped the principal with her work. It didn't get me out of doing my work, I still had to finish my work but I was going to a place where I could escape.

The one thing about middle school that I really **HATED,** (I barely use that word), was that my peers would make fun of me every day because I would wear the same green jacket to school. I liked the jacket, not so much for the design but I liked the comfort. Even at that young age, I didn't care what people thought about me *(well maybe I did a little bit).* The way you feel about yourself starts early in your life. It was something that I never talked about. You are not supposed to wear the same thing to school every day. Where did that come from? Who made that rule? What I find in life is that if you aren't careful, you will end up living your life based on other people's opinions. What a sad day it is when you choose to live according to what someone else thinks.

Let's talk about high school. These were the best days of my youth. I loved high school and often times I wish I could go back. I knew in the 9th grade that I wanted to produce stage plays. Being in front of people and performing was something that I found I loved.

I never will forget the first day I was the head anchor of the Fayette County High School News. I was in a broadcasting class with the intention of working behind the scenes with cameras. I was sitting in class one day doing a written classwork assignment. My teacher asked me to go get his mail in the front office. I enjoyed going to check the teacher's mailbox because it got me out of class. When I would go to check my teacher's mailbox, I should've gotten an award for "The Slowest Walk Ever." I took my time just so I could miss a large portion of the class. Anyway, I continued on to check his mail. I walked back in the classroom with a few magazines and a few envelopes. I turned the corner to walk in the classroom and there was a strange silence. I walked in and sat in my seat. As I was walking to my seat, I could sense everyone looking at me as if they wanted to burst out laughing. My teacher called my name and said "Johnnie, here is your chance to be on the morning announcements."

That moment changed my life. Baby *(In my New Orleans Voice)*, I ran around that classroom and even ran around out in the hallway. Everyone was looking at me as if I was crazy or crazier than they already thought. I finally calmed myself, read my notes and prepared myself to go LIVE for the first time. From that moment on Johnnie Busch was a household name.

I started out hosting the show about once a week. As popular demand grew I began hosting more often. I was simply being my authentic self. I started a portion of the program called "Words of Wisdom." I would encourage the entire school each day with small words of encouragement. The morning announcements made me famous. People would watch the program just to see what

I had to say. When God has a call on your life, you don't have to chase it. I didn't ask for it, I didn't beg for it, I didn't cheat to acquire the position. I walked through an open door that God had for me in that season.

I remember one time someone asked me to sign their dollar bill. I thought I was the biggest celebrity in that school. *(I actually was)* The lesson from elementary school to high school was that people treat you how they want to treat you but how you treat yourself is what matters. The ugly jacket I had on made me feel comfortable on the outside but terrible on the inside. The older I get I realize how I should treat myself with much respect and not worry what others will do or say. After all I'm Johnnie Busch.

"Good Morning this is Johnnie Busch and this is your morning announcements." From the morning announcements to live theatre, God knew actually where to place my footsteps.

I heard about a playwriting competition that the Drama Department was hosting. I was very interested in that competition. The object of the project was to write a one act play. I signed up right away. There were about 5 people in the entire school that entered the contest. I was extremely dedicated to this project. This was the first experience I ever had in writing a play. I never had any classes in playwriting. I've learned from experience.

I entered my play into the contest. The

play was entitled "A New Song." I was excited and hoping that I would win, but God knew best. There was a young girl by the name of "Waffle" that won the contest. Her nickname was waffle and her play was about washing dishes. I will not lie to you. I'm saying to myself here it is that I have a play about forgiveness and relationships with a powerful message. I'm not saying that she didn't deserve it, but I wanted it so bad. My drama teacher was one of the judges for that competition and he was excited that I joined the competition. I wasn't bitter for long because just a few years later, I went on to produce that very same stage play with over 700 people in attendance. I turned that 45-minute skit into a 2 hour play. God wasn't finish with me yet because years later my drama teacher inquired about auditioning for MY play. What? Did ya'll hear what I said? My drama teacher wanted to audition for my play. Who does that? That's favor, favor from the Lord. Congratulations to you Waffle on your award but I believe my waffle was just a bit sweeter. Can you pass the syrup please?

Chapter 3
I don't want to be Adult

James 1:2-4 Consider it all joy my brethren, when you encounter various trials, knowing that the testing of our faith produces endurance. And let endurance have its perfect result, so that you may be perfect and complete, lacking noting.

jdhjkdnnmdm647987680466bldbokdihdj47467djn bjdno646bndjkbnkdnojbndbnk67474odbndjdnbok ndfjb644yeyjoyjelkhrththrruryutyutyutyutyu dgjkbjdbdmkbokeiu3968903ibn9uryueuryuyruryn wgknknbgkwbkwg

No the above symbols are not in error. That is what it feels like sometimes when my alarm goes off. Sometimes life isn't fair but it is still good. That's why I feel it is important to obtain a career, something that you love. Now let me be the first to say that it is easier said than done.

Let's start with waking up in the morning. Now, that's only IF you are able to wake up in the morning. I say that because, a lot of people I find will be out partying all night and forget that they have responsibilities the next morning. I must say this, if you can hang out the night before and still get to your job *(on time)* then do so by all means. This is for those that can't. You know you better than anybody in this world. You may not want to admit certain personality traits but they are there. It's all about taking responsibility for our own lives. Often times *(Me included)* we fail to put first things first. If I have to be somewhere early in the morning, it is rare that you will see me out in the street the night before. The issue is not going out on a week night; the issue is not being able to maintain a job because you want to hang out. I feel strongly about this because I have many friends that put themselves in that situation. I think I need to say that again. We put ourselves in that situation. There is an old saying that states "A hard head will make a soft behind."

We learn from our own shortcomings. I'm the kind of person that if I am ever going through something, you just may never know. The warrior in me comes out every now and then. There have been many, many, many, many, times where I have not had a nickel. There have been times when my car was 24 hours away from being repossessed. There was a time when I almost got evicted. But God made a way for me to sustain my life so only he gets the glory. God made a way, financially for me to overcome those obstacles. Life's obstacles have a way of making you humble. What sense does it make for us to go through all of life's challenges and not learn a thing?

One of the biggest challenges that you may have as an adult is financial. I truly believe in saving for a rainy day. I always act broke, even when I'm not. Singer, songwriter, and Real Housewives of Atlanta Star Kandi Buress believes in living beneath your means. Just because you may have money to spend doesn't mean that you should necessarily spend it all the time. Being broke can be one of the best things that can happen to you.

I often say that we live in a microwave society. We want everything God has for us so quick. Often, we don't realize that God wants to give us everything we want and need; and everything that your heart desires, God can to give it to you. There is a scripture that supports what I'm saying. Psalms 37:4 reads "Delight yourself in the Lord and he will give you the desires of your heart."

I sometimes wish I was a kid again. I would stay a kid as long as I could. When you are a child, you wake up and feel the world is yours. You have no worries, you eat candy, take naps, and you play all day. What a life! Why do we have to grow up? Why do we have to become adults? I wish I knew those answers, but the truth of the matter is that being self-sufficient is one of the best feelings to have in the world.

I remember one Christmas I wanted my very own drum set. I'm not sure what my fascination of drums were but I wanted them really bad. I think it was all the noise I could make. I can't express how bad I wanted this drum set. I didn't have any lessons on how to play drums. I just thought I could naturally play. I woke up that Christmas morning with the smells of cinnamon rolls in the air. I was actually tired because I was up all night thinking about those drums or I could've been tired because every hour I would peek around the corner from the hallway to see if Santa Clause put my special gift under the tree. I walked into the living room and continued to look around. I did not see a drum set. I opened all off my other gifts. I must say that I was happy for all the other gifts but was looking for my drums. Truthfully, if I had just received the drums. I would be happy. If I had gotten the drums I would probably only use them for just a few weeks. I would still be using the drums to this day even if I had to pay for it. We tend to take care of things longer if we actually buy them ourselves. *True*

I moved out on my own at the age of 23. I was not financially ready to move, but I believed if I were to stay in that mindset I would've never moved. Financial stability really hit home when I moved out. Being broke can be one of the most depressing things ever. I've been broke plenty of times as I mentioned before. I never had a handle on my finances. There was no structure in my life with my money. I was the king of extensions. It got so bad that I would forget what day to pay who and then I would get another extension for the extension that I already had. Can I get a witness right now? I didn't really have a plan for my finances. If you eat in your 30's then you will starve in your 50's. Money management is really important in one's life.

Many people want the blessings of God to rain down on their financial situation. We get our priorities mixed up. You don't need a financial miracle, you need money, and that comes from a job, and that comes with gifts or talent. It all starts with an idea. Ask yourself, what you're thinking about? Again, it all starts with an idea. Think about it, you are working for someone that had a idea. What makes you so different? You don't need a miracle to pay your bills, you need a job.

I would go out to eat, shop, overcharge credit cards and not think twice about it. I was doing all that and putting $5 in the tithes and offering bucket and I actually thought I was sacrificing if I did $10. Don't let the pastor ask for $11, I would cringe or just go to the bathroom. I was really struggling. I mixed up being frugal with disobedience. I would just buy the things that I wanted and begged for the things that I need.

People think that just because you have produced several stage plays doesn't mean that you are rich. The more you have the more responsibilities you have. It takes a while to truly manage money. I've held down a 9-5 while producing shows, managing artists, and going to school full time. You either make money or let the money make you. I didn't want to live my life just to pay bills. Who wants to do that? That isn't fun. A motto that I try to live by is, if I can't buy it twice then I don't buy it. Money is important; money affords you a lot of things; money is nice; but money is not everything. Create a plan, build a budget and let your money work for you. Some days I don't want to be adult but I have no choice. UGH!

Chapter 4
Role Call
(I love Theatre)

Exodus 9:16 But I have raised you up for this very purpose, that I might show you my power and that my name might be proclaimed in all the earth.

Writer, Director, Producer Tyler Perry has been one of my biggest influences for theatre. He is by far the main reason I am in the theatre industry today. Tyler Perry's rise from a homeless individual to a multi-millionaire makes me want to run just right there. I rose from theatre straight from the classroom. The classroom was my stage. I loved going to school, not for the work but to simply have a good time and make people laugh. When I watch Tyler Perry I often see bits and pieces of him in me. There is nothing better for me than seeing an audience watching something that you created. The creators of stage have been around before my lifetime. There were many other pioneers when it comes to breaking ground in the theatre business. Maya Angelou, August Wilson, and Lorraine Hansberry. Ms. Hansberry was the first black woman to write a play and perform on Broadway. That is incredible. I'm a student of life. I observe all things surrounding me. I pay attention to people's life and I admire the fact that I can possibly walk in their footsteps.

My journey of writing started in high

school. One beautiful afternoon when everyone else was playing basketball, walking, running, or on their cell phones, I was writing. I wrote a play that became my first production entitled "A New Song." I knew at that very moment that it would become a reality. I may be the biggest procrastinator that you may have ever known. The fact that I actually sat down with a pen a paper was a huge compliment for me. I can't even express how that moment has changed my life. I made a decision to complete a task.

I produced my first play in 2008. The play was entitled "A New Song." I was the youngest, and the first African American to produce a stage play on my own in the Atlanta area according to a local county newspaper. I rented out what was once Fayetteville's first movie theatre. I was the first person to produce a play in that venue. Since then, many productions have been produced in that theatre. Opening night might have been one of the scariest moments in my life. Luckily for us we had a packed house each night. The crowd wasn't an issue, thank God. I was hoping and praying that the audience would openly receive my content. I had many friends and family in the audience on those days. The days leading up to the production were a tremendous undertaking. Keep in mind that I was still in school and I still had to make good grades while doing a production. It was difficult but I knew it could be completed. I knew God had called me for such a time as this.

Let's talk about the process for a production. It all starts with a well thought out script. After I completed the script I went on a major hunt to locate a venue. I traveled near and far for the perfect spot. The amazing thing that I love about that is that God already knew where the production would be held. I've searched all over and finally found the right place. After the venue was found I then started to hold auditions at local churches and the local library. *(Side note: I've had several productions. At this time I won't go through each production's experience so don't worry.)* I no longer hold auditions anymore but to my surprise from that day to this, God has blessed me to have close to over 300 people audition. The audition process takes a lot of time but it is well worth it. The talent that I saw coming through those doors were nothing short of amazing. I often say I now know how the judges felt on American Idol. To be completely honest, there were times when I wanted to laugh out loud. As silly as I am, an outburst was just seconds away. Some people really thought they could sing but my ears thought different. I know I can't sing so I don't even try. Many people would come out from my school and many from the community. We advertised auditions everywhere possible. We were all over the city. Year after year the crowd that came to audition grew to amazing numbers. That is the power of promotion.

After the auditions, my team and I had to set rehearsal schedules. Also keep in mind that the actors at that time were strictly volunteering so the dedication was definitely there. I saw the passion from their hearts each night at rehearsals. The rehearsals were only a couple days of week but my team worked hard to present the best production possible. As we approached the opening date of the shows, the rehearsals were intense.

Let me just stop right now and say thank you every actor, usher, band member, camera operator, and anyone that had anything to do with my productions. I sincerely thank you from the bottom of my heart. All of you have worked tirelessly to make sure that my vision came to pass. I would not have done it without you. You have made me a better person. You have given me a stronger work ethic. I just had to say thank you because I truly am grateful for all that you have taught me in life.

Ok! Let's get back to the process. The script has been written, the venue has been found, the auditions are over, the rehearsals have come to an end and now it is opening night. The smell of popcorn fills the air. The seats are filling up. The audiences are chattering in anticipation. While those lovely things are happening inside the lobby and the Theatre, I'm backstage sweating like Donald Trump in a Soul Food Cafeteria. I've prayed the night before to make sure that everything would be a success and here I am walking the floor and worrying about everything. It's just like us to worry when God has already given us an assurance that everything will be alright. I've heard it said that if you are going to worry then don't pray. It defeats the purpose.

Lights come up and it's show time. The seats are filled and the actors are in character and ready to entertain and inspire our audience. Everything was going great. The sound was good, the audience was laughing, the actors were visible and the message was being brought and now here comes the horror story. I was NOT ready for what was about to come. About roughly 20-30 minutes into the show I get a phone call. I did not want to receive this phone call but it had to happen. I was actually backstage when I received the phone call that one of my actors could not be a part of the show. The original plan was for him leave his baseball game at halftime so he could make it in time for his role. As life would have it, he broke his finger in the middle of the baseball game. It probably wasn't even a good idea on my part to agree to have him to participate for that night. Keep in mind we had two other shows. Therefore, he was able to be in the show. He was unable to arrive at the theatre on time because he was forced to go to the emergency room.

I didn't have a understudy, that was my first mistake. I am walking back and forth backstage trying to figure out what to do. There was only one thing to do and that would be for me to go onstage. I wasn't planning on going onstage until the end of the show to thank the people for coming. I had on a red dress shirt and black dress pants. His character was that of a thug, that of which is far from my personality. I untucked my dress shirt and rolled up one pants leg. I went out there and played his part throughout the entire show. The cast and I finally made it to the end. We were all scared and didn't know what to do. After we thanked the audience and took our bows, he came walking backstage right when it was all over. Everyone huddled around him to make sure that he was ok.

It was unbelievable that he would come right after the show, to the second. It wasn't his fault, he has no control over what happened but I was glad he took care of himself. That night could've easily been called Friday the 13th. My cast played their parts and the audience NEVER knew *(Until today)* that I was never supposed to be in that show. It was one of the scariest moments, but life lessons were learned.

I shared the experiences with a few people and some of the comments were alarming.

"Why didn't you have an understudy"?

"Why did you encourage or allow one of your actors to participate in a baseball game the same night as a performance?"

"Wasn't it easy, since you wrote the play?"

Let me answer the first question. I didn't have an understudy because I didn't know I needed one. I was still learning the process. After all, it was my first play. I now understand the importance of having backup. Anything could happen, so any production definitely needs understudies. I thought that the actor would be at the theatre on time. I had faith in him. Neither of us expected his finger to break. I agreed not knowing of any possible causes that would prevent him from participating.

Writing a play doesn't necessarily mean that you know the entire story. Some people were suggesting that I should've known his part word for word since I wrote it. My response to that is, I not only wrote his part but 16 other parts as well. I guessed all the way through the show. I was more nervous and really couldn't think straight. I've definitely learned how to facilitate better productions. I had to learn the hard way but I thank God I learned the lesson. To this day, I still love theatre. That's why I know I'm put on this earth to write stories because I still love it. That situation didn't stop me from doing anything. Theatre is my life; I love it. I love sharing stories while inspiring people. I now have found a love for promotions.

I have several artists that I promote and I love the fact that I can mentor them in any way possible. I also picked up a love for organizing events. I'm glad and honored God gave me all these talents. I'm using these gifts every day. I thank God for my career, I thank God for my life, and I thank God for you. As you start your day begin to just simply thank God for who he is. Don't ask for anything, just thank him. Thank him for his kindness, thank him for his love, let's thank him for his peace that he has given us so we can live as he would have us. God has given us everything we need to be successful. It's up to us to make that change. We are so consumed with people and opinions and the everyday difficulties of life that we often don't live in our full potential. I found my love for theatre and God has filled this house every since.

Chapter 5
Bishop Busch

Mark 16:15 And he said unto them, go ye into all the world, and preach the Gospel to every creature.

"Won't God Do It?" and "Yes God Will" is just not a part of my T- Shirt line but it is my testimony. My faith in God has been a major part of my life. God is truly the author and finisher of this book. He is my everything. I want to make it very clear that I don't pray to the universe or to the atmosphere as some others would claim, but I believe in God. How would you describe God? Yes, YOU. How would you describe him? Well, for me he is my everything. I don't just call on him when I need him but I call on him even when I think I have everything. My faith gets me through all of the hard times. My faith is even giving me the courage to finish this book.

I believe in daily affirmations. My daily prayer for years has been the prayer of Jabez. The Prayer of Jabez comes from the Bible. In 1 Chronicles 4:10, we read: *"And Jabez called on the God of Israel, saying, Oh that Thou wouldest bless me indeed, and enlarge my coast, and that Thine hand might be with me, and that Thou wouldest keep me from evil, that it may not grieve me! And God granted him that which he requested."* The prayer is composed of four parts. First, Jabez asks God to bless him. Second, he asks God to enlarge his territory or increase his responsibility. Third, he prays that God will be with him and stay close. Lastly, Jabez asks that God keep him from harm so that he will be free from pain. My favorite part of the prayer is God enlarging my territory. The prayer of Jabez simply means to me that everywhere I walk in this life that God is with me. God is covering me. God is taking care of me. I know that the prayer is being manifested in my life when I can't explain God's blessing. People often ask me *(people really do ask me so its not just not a cliché)* "How did that happen to you?" I explain an act of God by not explaining it at all. When you can't explain how it happens to you then that's a good indicator that God has worked in your favor. Amen!

Let me give you an example. Just a few

years ago I was always fascinated about working at a hotel. I don't know why. The hospitality industry began to become very interesting to me. After working at a fast food restaurant and as a security guard, I finally applied at a local hotel and I got the job. Keep in mind that I APPLIED, that means I was LOOKING for a job. I'll tell you why that's important in a second. I applied, went for the interview and I got the job. Those were the best 2 ½ years of my life. I learned so much about the industry. I never knew that it was preparing me for bigger things. The hotel where I was working at was a 99 room property. Hold on, the shouting moment is coming. So I was going to work faithfully every day. I was married to the 3-11p.m. shift. I met some great people who I still talk to today. I wouldn't take anything for my journey. And then there was God…. In the midst of working a full time job I was still producing stage plays. I was teaching theatre workshops and I was looking for a place to host a banquet. I drove all over Atlanta to find the perfect venue to host my function. I finally walked into this beautiful 378 room hotel. I walked in and greeted the front desk agent who then got in contact with a salesperson that would help me secure a room for my event. I finally waited patiently for the sales manager. The friendly sales manager finally came to greet me and assist. We walked over to another part of the lobby and briefly discussed what I was looking for. Ya'll I didn't know my blessing was a few minutes away. We saw a few rooms and ended the meeting. I told her that I would be in contact with her shortly. I then went to the restroom. As I walked out she approached me, she said "Are you looking for a job?" "I think you may be a great fit. I replied "not really." I was already employed and comfortable. The sales manager said "I think you should just give it a try and see what happens." She then called down to human resources and scheduled me for a interview. In about 20 minutes of an interview process and negotiating, I found out I had gotten the job. I need ya'll to shout right there, but don't throw my book across your bedroom. Put my book down and then shout. The moral of the story is favor isn't fair. I walked in for something else and I walked out with a job. I didn't apply

Amen !.

and I wasn't looking. It followed me, his grace and mercy followed me, his love, followed me. His loving angels follow me as I follow him. That was a moment that to this day I cannot explain. I love telling that story because God has showed me that day that he will never leave me alone. Keep your daily routine going because when it's for you, it's for you.

It's not about me but it's all about Jesus. Every person I come in contact with I want them to know the same God I serve. My prayer life has drastically increased. Every situation I have encountered, I prayed my way through it. We go through things in life not always for us but for other people. God's light has to shine through us. Take time to find your quiet space.

That's right

There comes a time in your life, when you walk away from all the drama and people who create it. You surround yourself with people who make you laugh. Forget the bad, and focus on the good. Love the people who treat you right, pray for the ones who don't. Life is too short to be anything but happy. Falling down is a part of life; getting back up is living. – Jose N. Harris

This chapter maybe the shortest chapter in the book, not because God hasn't done enough, its because I just can't explain it.

Chapter 6
Before you Walk Down
the aisle, take a nap

Mark 10:6-9 "But at the beginning of creation God made them male and female. For this reason a man will leave his father and mother to be united to his wife, and the two will become one flesh. So they are no longer two, but one flesh. Therefore what God has joined together, let no one separate.

W hy aren't you? When Will you? Why haven't you? Have you?

All those are questions that I receive on a daily basis. With all those questions, not one time has anyone asked, "Are you happy?" Let me explain.

My prayer for every person on this earth is to find their own happiness. You maybe wondering what this chapter is about. This is my chapter solely on relationships. I named this chapter "Before you walk down the aisle, take a nap." We often feel better after we take a nap. We tend to make better decisions when we are well rested. Any decision is better made when you have the capacity to do so. I believe before walking into a relationship you have to be complete with yourself. So many times, so many people seek others to complete them. If you aren't complete with yourself then you can't fully be complete with someone else.

One of my favorite actresses and comediennes is Whoppi Goldberg. I could watch her movie "Sister Act" all day long. Ms. Goldberg has a book titled "If Someone Says You Complete Me, Run." I love the title alone. No one can complete you but you. Ok! I think I've said that enough.

Let's get personal for a few minutes. I am a single guy. I love myself and everything about it. I am complete within myself. In this day and age you cannot be single and happy and not be criticized. People have made up in their minds their assumption of you without even having a conversation with you. If you are single, if you were raised around women, and if you are a Theatre Geek then you must be gay. What? Really? I've been called that several times. The part that has frustrated me for a long time was the fact that people are slick when it comes to their conversation. The questions would be "Are you dating?" "Do you have a girlfriend?" "Why don't you have a girlfriend?" The list goes on and on. They ask all those questions to cover up the question they really want to ask. "Are you gay?" I would prefer you ask me that than all the other questions, because you don't really care about anything else. I've been getting those questions for a long time so I'm used to it. They think they are reading me but I can read them from a mile away. I would prefer that people be upfront and honest.

I also choose to keep my private life personal. And some of you reading this may be wondering well, "He hasn't even answered the question yet?" That's all some think about. The best way to keep a relationship honest is to not advertise it. The best relationships are the ones when nobody knows. I've been married now for the past 5 years. I first met him back in 1977 at the Piggly Wiggly in Augusta, Georgia. No, I'm seriously joking. When I do settle down and find the right woman, only a few people will know. Those that I feel actually care will be the ones to know. People will still have their own assumptions regardless. I'm looking forward to a relationship sooner or later with a woman that God has for me.

I firmly believe that marriage is supposed to be between a man and a woman. We have to do better as a community when it comes to judgment. How can we save the world if we condemn their actions? For the record, I have many gay friends, straight friends, crazy friends. I don't care who you are or your background. I can still call you my friend. We have been taught that a homosexual lifestyle is wrong. The homosexual lifestyle is not pleasing in Gods eyes. We should be the change in the world and love those who may not love like us.

Love is very important in one's life. Many of us will sacrifice anything just to have someone in their life. Many of you that are reading this book right now are putting up with your significant other. The minute you find a better job, you have already made up in your mind that you are leaving him/her. Repeat this aloud, "I will not settle for anything less than God's best." Let that be your declaration.

Marriage is also supposed to be a lifetime commitment. That's means you should be with your partner for the rest of your life. Till death do you part! Before you decide if you want to marry someone, make a list of five things that you dislike about that person. How many of those things can you live with? As for me I'm petty, I have to get used to living with someone for the rest of my life. I like certain things in certain places. I like the air on a certain temperature. Sometimes I like to sleep with music and so forth. I guess I will deal with that later on down the road. I would recommend looking for perfect but look for someone who can complement you.

Having a significant other can help you grow into being a better person. You may not see certain flaws until it is pointed out. Marriage can be great when you mutually have a good understanding of each other. For the Bible says "She that finds a husband find it good and obtains favor with the Lord." Now God said, Oh wait! I think I quoted that wrong, hold on let me google the correct version. Ok. The Bible says 'He who finds a wife finds what is good and obtains favor from the Lord." I want all the favor that I can get. For all of my men out there, don't get married just so you can obtain favor. If you get anything out of this chapter I would want it to be that God has shined his light on you. You have the power to have the best relationship in the world. Observe others, read books, talk to God, and let him guide you. He will never steer you wrong. Even if God did steer me wrong, I still would want to go wherever he is.

Also when it comes to relationships, take your time. Please take your time. Why is everything a rush? We live in a microwave society. We want everything quick.

We wake up

Rush a quick prayer (That's if you do pray)

Rush to brush your teeth (If you have any)

Rush the kids to get ready for school

Run Red Lights to get to work

Rush your workload, just to clock out

Rush to pick up the kids

Rush to get home

Rush babysitter over

Rush to get ready for your date

Rush your date over to your house because you are late

Rush to the restaurant

Rush to eat

Rushing back home

Going to sleep and doing the same routine all over again.

Today I encourage you to slow down. We chase love when love is supposed to chase us.

Have you ever had love chase you? I can write an entire play on marriage and I've never been married. I've witnessed a lot in relationships and I have come to the fact that I want to be happy. I realize there will be ups and downs and many heartaches. But I claim the best relationship status to overtake you and me. We will thrive and love our spouse that way that God intended.

Don't rush yourself. We put the load on us because of people's expectations. From the words of the singer Fantasia, I recommend you to "Free Yourself." Let me free you from this. People will have an opinion on your life as long as the day is long. You can't live your life based on what someone thinks. If you stay single, then they talk. If you get married then they talk. It is better to do what you feel is right. I won't ask you "Are you married?", or Are you dating?" At the end of the day my prayer is for you is for you to be happy. "Are you happy?" "Are you at peace?"

A relationship is ordained by God. Why would we let something that has been ordained by God be ordained by someone else? Let's get back to the place of trusting God, loving God, talking to God. I believe you must have a relationship with God first, then yourself, then your significant other, in that order. Don't put so much energy in trying to figure out what people are thinking. Put that energy in loving God, loving yourself and then loving your mate. We often say that God is love. After reading this chapter I want you to feel empowered when it comes to making better decisions about your relationships. There's an old song that says "Get your house in order." Whenever you need to make an important decision in life, I encourage you to take a nap. Not necessarily a physical nap, but an emotional nap. After you take a nap, you will feel so much better. Before you say "I DO", turn down the lights and say Goodnight.

Let this change your life.

God can change your life, if you let him.

Let God use you, everybody else has.

Chapter 7
Eat the cheese,
Pray about it and die

Romans 3:23 "for all have sinned and fall short of

the glory of God."

This chapter is about making the best decisions in our everyday lives. When I think about Cheese and all that he has done for me, my soul cries out halleluiah. My name is Johnnie Busch and I like cheese. I like soda. I like fried foods and I like pasta. I like each one of those items mentioned, but overtime having them in abundance can ultimately harm your body. Why can't we enjoy the things that we love? Why can't we eat the foods that we love? Why? Why? Why? Many people have questioned the title of this chapter in regards to them not knowing what it means.

Many of us know what's right and what's wrong. I heard famed Poet Maya Angelou say that "When you know better, you do better." We don't want to go to the gym. We don't want to eat healthier. We don't want to invest in a savings account. We just don't want to do it. We can be some of the worst procrastinators ever.

Hence the title:

Eat the cheese, knowing it's bad for you

Pray about it, thinking that you can still eat the bad apple and prosper.

Die, you die, you fail, you defeat your purpose.

We know what's good for us but we don't follow it through. You can't hope that you will receive positive outcomes when you are not doing what it takes to fulfill your vision. This book has been a couple of years in the making. You would not be reading this book if I had not put pen to paper. I put away the dead thing that was holding me back which was procrastination. I was procrastinating, praying that God would give me vision for the book after he already gave it to me. Let's pause right there. God has already GIVEN you what you need. We hold on to what we think we want. We have to be willing to let go of our plans and grab a hold of what God has for our lives. *What is your deadweight? What is holding you back? What is your cheese? What is your soda? Can you identify what is holding you back?* It may be the thing that can save your life.

Patience is one thing that I have learned to acquire. I get invited to a lot of church events and programs and I'm often escorted to the front. For a long time, I did not want to sit in the front. Many people would question me with why I didn't want to sit in the front. One usher insisted that I sit up front. I told her "no thank you." God was teaching me that it was NOT about me. So many times when people sit up front they love to be seen, they want everyone to see them and see how important they are. I've been there and done that. Long story short, God was teaching me that it was not about me. I was learning that I needed to sit in the back for a season. It wasn't so much the physical aspect of being seated in the front, but it was a mindset that I got away from. The whole reason I'm alive is to serve and be obedient until God was ready to bring me to the front. My cheese or my deadweight was being obedient. I knew I heard God's voice. The usher didn't understand because God didn't speak to her, he spoke to me. When God gives you a task, you must fulfill it. It's not for him but it's for you.

The reason I keep mentioning cheese is because I love it. The result of my cheese addiction maybe what has caused my high blood pressure. I was diagnosed with high blood pressure at the young age of eighteen. As I'm writing this book I struggle with eating properly and exercising on a regular basis. But glory be to God just some time ago I found me a personal trainer and Glory to be to God I'm on the right path to a healthier body. I hope my doctor isn't reading this book because I haven't been taking my medicine. That's right, I have not been taking it lately. I know I should be, but being hardheaded, I stopped. By the time you get this book, I would be taking my medicine and exercising daily and occasionally passing by Popeye's and American Deli. I didn't want to make this chapter about food and health but it's beginning to be that way. Since I'm on the topic of food. Let's talk about a few tips on cooking.

I love to cook. I don't cook as much as I

would like to but I do know how. After all women do like men that can cook. (Smiling) When it comes to cooking I use "Light Salt" it is usually found in a blue container. That helps you from putting extra salt on your food. It tastes just like salt but it has less sodium. Grilled chicken, salmon, salad and many vegetables are obviously good for you. Again, we all KNOW that but we choose other options. I realized I can't eat what I want, pray about it and then die or fail myself in the end.

Everything in life has precautions and consequences. I will never forget many years ago when I was at my Aunt's house in South Atlanta. I loved going to her house in the summer months because I knew I could count on a good meal. If I couldn't count on anything else, I could count on a good meal. We would either go out to eat or she would cook. This particular night we made it simple and we chose, or I chose rather to cook Hamburger Helper. I believe this may have been my first time cooking it.

My aunt was upstairs looking though papers. Every time I came over to her house she always had a project for me. Cleaning, reorganizing, climbing to the roof, crawling through the basement, painting the house and even walking to Jerusalem with a half of glass of water. I'm joking, she is really great. She came downstairs to make sure that I didn't burn down her kitchen. I was browning the ground beef. The next step was to combine the sauce mix with the milk. I swore up and down that the recipe needed more milk. Little did I know that the milk thickens after you mix it with the sauce. My family nickname is JR and I distinctly remember that she said "JR, people have tested that recipe. The instructions on the box are there to help you. They know what they are doing." It's funny how certain things stick with you. She may have forgotten but I still remember that moment. One thing about my Aunt is that she won't make you do anything, she will tell you and then it's up to you. I listened and it turned out great. I calmly hear God telling us to LISTEN and it will turn out GREAT.

If you just stop and be honest with yourself. You know the right thing to do when it comes to your health. The wrong choices can often lead us into place where we don't want to be. I'm reminded when I was at a very young age *(can't recall the age).* I was always interested in cooking. I've watched family members for so long and I have found a love in preparing meals. My cousin turned the stove on that particular evening and we both knew that it was very hot. The inquisitive person that I was, I decided to touch the hot stove.

If I was baptized back then I would have called on the Father, the Son, and the Holy Ghost. I burned my hand and screamed to the end of days. Not only did I get burned as if that wasn't punishment enough, I also got beaten by a family member that same night. If you ask me, double punishment was not needed. I repeat, it was not needed at all. I knew it was hot but I decided to touch it anyway. Shame on me. I learned the hard way. God sometimes put us in situations to test us. I often say that we are currently still in certain situations because we have not learned the lesson yet.

Think about your life, think about where you want to be. What we think and what God thinks are two different things. You keep telling yourself that you have lost a lot of weight but if you turn around and look behind you, you will find the rest of it. You are telling your husband you can cook but you don't know that when you go to sleep he goes down to the kitchen to eat Popeye's that he brought on the way home from work. You want to cast out demons for your girlfriends husband and you can't even kill a roach in your own house. YOU DON'T HAVE ANY POWER!

Do you see what I'm saying? I see you shaking you head. You haven't learned the lesson. You are where you are because you haven't learned the lesson. When you have passed the test then you will go on the next test. Keep in mind the test never stops. They just keep getting greater and greater. Find you battle, find your lesson. Don't eat the cheese, pray about it and then die. Choose life and choose it today!

Chapter 8
Pay attention to your life

Job 36:11 "If they hear and serve him, they

will end their days in prosperity and their years in

pleasures"

We as a people tend to pay attention to everyone and everything else besides what is important. We have more to say about somebody else's life and our own life is in a pickle. This chapter I've chosen to take some life lessons from the legendary Maya Angelou.

"If you don't like something, change it. If you can't change it, change your attitude."

Your life is yours to live. If you are truly happy with your life, then I applaud you. Change is a part of life. Change is something that you must go through in life. I believe there is such a thing as bad change. Bad change is when you change someone for your good and your good only. No matter how hard you try, you are wasting your time trying to change someone. I bet if you change your attitude about how you see your life, you would be in a better place.

"When someone shows you who they are, believe them the first time."

Where are you right now? No, seriously. I'm asking, where are you while you are reading this book? Are you in your bedroom? I'm sure you can look up and see a T.V. around somewhere? Are you riding in the car? I'm sure you can see buildings or trees? Are you out on your back porch? I'm sure you can see a calming lake or the soft presence of fresh green grass. Whatever object you see, I guarantee you that an object is just an object. My point is a T.V. is a T.V. Grass is grass. A building is a building. If someone lies to you, then believe it. If someone gossips about you behind your back, then believe it. Believe what you see for what it is. This also goes back to changing people. If it acts like a duck, quacks like a duck then it's a duck. Believe what you see the first time. One thing when it comes to gossip, there's a saying that says "Believe none of what you hear and half of what you see." What chu looking at? How u doing? How u feeling? Believe it!!!

"My mission in life is not merely to survive, but to thrive; and to do so with some passion, some compassion, some humor, and some style.

Every one of us should have a mission in life. Even when you are on your job, there is a mission, a goal, a purpose. Whatever you find yourself doing, do it and do it to its fullest. Food makes me happy. When I'm eating something GOOD, I dance, shake my feet a little bit, and sometimes I will sing. Can I get a witness? Food makes me happy. I can be driving somewhere and I can have the right song on and I'm dancing all the way. I'm not only doing certain things but I thriving. I'm living every moment to the fullest. I love others hard. I genuinely care about others. I work hard, play hard, and love hard. I also live life with humor, sometimes a little too much humor. Humor is what makes the world go around. So many times we make things more serious than they ought to be. I'm the kind of person that you do not want to sit next to during a funeral. I will find something humorous in that setting. Find your mission, thrive, and laugh until it hurts. It gets better. Pay attention to your life, it costs you less.

Chapter 9
I'm weird but it's OK!

__1 Peter 4:10-11__ "As every man hath received the gift, even so minister the same one to another, as good stewards of the manifold grace of God. If any man speaks, let him speak as the oracles of God; if any man minister, let him do it as of the ability which God giveth: that God in all things may be glorified through Jesus Christ, to whom be praise and dominion for ever and ever. Amen.

I'm weird but it's ok. I'm embarrassed so I will share just a few.

- I count how many times I brush my hair. I make sure each side has the same amount of brushes.

- I sometimes sleep naked. I have pictures on the next page.

- I like all cold drinks with ice. (I HATE room temperature drinking water.)

- I always fill my car up when the gauge lands on "E".

- I do certain things on a time frame. For example, I may be watching TV and want something to drink, I will go on the hour or half hour or 15 and 45 of the clock, just because of the time.   The time determines when I go.

- Every time I go to the movies I go to a different theatre. (Just for the experience of new places)

O.k. I've shared enough. I'm weird but it's ok. I LOVE being different, I LOVE being weird. The more people question it, the more comfortable I get. One thing is for sure I'm living as I would have it. I've come to believe that weird things or acts aren't really weird things. The purpose of this chapter is to make you feel more comfortable. Nowadays the weird things have become normal things. Don't be depressed, or in denial. Live in your truth, and if it's weird, it's ok.

Romans 12:2 reads "Do not be conformed to this world, but be transformed by the renewal of your mind, that by testing you may discern what is the will of God, what is good and acceptable and perfect."

One of my favorite parts of that scripture is "Do not be conformed to this world." The world conforms means to behave accordingly to socially acceptable conventions or standards. The world does a lot of things that Christians or believers may call weird and the world thinks that Christians are weird. I use the example that the world is going to do what they are going to do regardless. So why not live your life as if God would have it. Live a life pleasing to God and God only. I'd rather be weird with God than normal with people. Get to the point where you can be satisfied with God and God only. Being weird is a title, a title that someone can put on you. Just as they put it on, you can take it off. Renew your mind and let go.

Jeremiah 1:5 reads, "Before I formed you in the womb I knew you, and before you were born I consecrated you; I appointed you a prophet to the nations."

BEFORE God formed us, he knew us. Can you meet a stranger on the street today and comfortably say that you already knew them? No. You can't. That's the amazing thing about God, he knew us before we knew ourselves. Sometimes I sit back and think about how good God has been to me. He knew that I was going to cuss out that lady in traffic. He knew that I was going leave the buggy in the parking lot instead of the appropriate buggy area. He knew that I would drink that can of soda when I should be drinking water. He knows it all. He knows our next breath. I think that God had a sense of humor when he created me. I'm far from normal and I LOVE it. I LOVE who I am. I LOVE weird things. At the end of the day, it doesn't matter what anyone THINKS. What does God THINK? What is in that blessed book? We mess ourselves up when we ask for opinions. Why? The next time you need some advice, open your Bible. The answers are there and the reward will be great. God knew us and he knew we were going to need him. He appointed us to be a servant. Who are you serving today?

John 15:19 "If you were of the world, the world would love you as its own; but because you are not of the world, but I chose you out of the world, therefore the world hates you.

We are in this world but not of the world. It's ok to not fit in. It's ok to be a little weird. This chapter is for those that always feel out of place or feel that no one agrees with you. Just as sure as I'm writing this book, I hear you and know that God is with you. Remember when I said that God knew us before we were even born? He knew we were going to be different in the world's eyes. The amazing thing is that the world can be just like us. He chose us out of he world to be a representative for him. The world may hate us, but God loves us. I look at the world today and see all the hate. Where has that gotten us? Nowhere. You win by love. Let's show the world the opposite of what they are doing.

Psalms 139:14 "I praise you, for I am fearfully and wonderfully made. Wonderful are your works; my soul knows it very well.

I think this scripture fits this chapter the best. We are fearfully and wonderfully made. This scripture tell us that we should not be normal. It's time to step out of your comfort zone and be what God has called you to be. We should walk without fear. We should see ourselves the way that God sees us. We are wondrous in his eyes. His work is wonderful. My soul knows it very well. I thank God for my life. I thank God for my experience. I'm glad to be what the world calls weird. I'm going to say it again. I absolutely love it. I want you to LOVE the skin that you are in. LOVE what you look like. LOVE who you are. LOVE your flaws. LOVE your opinions and your way of thinking. LOVE yourself. You are a child of the highest king. You are fearfully and wonderfully made. You are above and not beneath. Your finances are coming in order. You career is about to be birthed. Your book is about to be written. You have everything you need to be great. Your happiness is NOT for sale. You are weird but it's ok.

Chapter 10
I'm FINE and YOU?

1 Samuel 16:7 "But the LORD said to Samuel, "Do

not look on his appearance or on the height of his

stature, because I have rejected him. For

the LORD sees not as man sees: man looks on the

outward appearance, but the LORD looks on the

heart."

Thank you hanging in there with me. We have come to an end. First, let me explain how the title came about. Sometimes when you meet people you never know how long you will be friends. I've been working in the hospitality industry for a few years now and I met a friend. Her name was Ms. Gordon. I will leave it at that. When I first met her I didn't like her at all. We bumped heads. We never got along. But, it brought great joy to my eyes every time I saw her name on the schedule. She was one of those people that will knock you out and then take you to the hospital. As any job would have it, you have your crazy fun times and your serious professional times. We would be as random as possible. We would make each other laugh to the point where our stomach hurts. (No, she's not dead so don't think I'm setting that up) I couldn't even explain all the crazy things we did, because you just wouldn't understand.

One afternoon, I can't remember exactly what I said but she turned around with QUICKNESS and said "I'm Fine and You." You had to be there to laugh at that statement. That saying came from a place of concern. I guess. So many times we ask people how are they doing and don't wait for a response. I'd rather you just say "Good Morning", "Good Afternoon" or "Good Evening." If you are truly concerned about how someone is doing, please wait for a response and then genuinely proceed. If you don't care about how someone is feeling or you're not in the mood then just simply say hello. So, "I'm Fine and You" is a response to how well you actually care about someone. Nowadays I will just randomly say it. Someone may have an opinion about your life. I'm fine and you. You hear something about someone you know and you don't want to bring on negative energy. I'm fine and you. Everyone around you is not having a good day and they try and bring you down. I'm fine and you.

No one on this earth can tell you how you feel but you. I dislike when I'm invited over someone's house and they ask me if I want something to drink and I reply "no, thank you" and they insist that I have something to drink. In my mind I'm thinking, "Why do I have to have something to drink just because you're thirsty?" Like for real? I know if I'm hungry or thirsty. People actually get offended that you don't take them up on their offers. I've heard it said that it was rude not to take a gift when someone offered it to you. Well, I have to say I think it's rude to take something and then not use it. It's a waste. People will walk up to me and ask, "Do you want this cake?" or "Do you want this piece of candy?

Why is it that you don't want it? Are you really giving me a gift? Don't RE-GIFT me. I'm not a recycle bin.

We place pressure on people when it comes to marriage. You don't' have kids and they say something is wrong with you. You have one child and they say, when are you having another? You have three kids and they say you have too many. We place pressure on finances. You bought a Honda. They said you should've bought a Toyota. We place pressure on what people wear; where we go to church, what we eat. When will we get to the point where we take care of ourselves? Words of advice if someone doesn't ask for your opinion then don't give it to them because and opinion is just an opinion. Now, I'm not talking about advice. That's different. Sometimes people do need to know that what they are doing is hurting them and eventually they would need to stop. But when it comes to things that are based on an opinion, I believe that should cease.

I never met a person that I wanted to change. I live my life in hopes that you would see the Glory of God as my testimony.

As for me I'm good, I'm fine. I'm content and happy with my life. I know who I am and I know whose I am. This life is not about us but it's about who we can inspire and uplift. We all have hard times but it's not about how you fall it's about how you get up.

Don't discount the people that you meet along the way. I have met some crazy, interesting people along the way. I would not be who I am today if I have not embraced every relationship. You can pick and choose what you are willing to learn from someone.

I've had a few people that I've met along the way that I am just forever grateful for. Ms. Moochie is her name. I love her. She has encouraged me to finish this book and randomly would check up on me to see how far I've gotten. You ever met someone that is there for you no matter what? We are like Oprah and Gayle, Bonnie and Clyde, Bill Cosby and Clair. The reason I adore her so much is because she is just as honest as she is silly. Anyone that can make me laugh and be beyond silly is alright with me. You all can truly tell that I truly LIVE every day without any regret. She is always full of life and always willing to listen when I rant about different things. I love you and all the fun times we have had thus far. Oh and Moochie, "Sometimes you gotta MIXXXXX IT UPPPPPPP." (Inside joke)

I want everyone to know that I could not write about every single person. If you do not see your name listed please refer to the introduction page where I generically list and thank everyone. Don't email me talking about why your name wasn't in the book and the last time we talked was Thanksgiving of '78.

When you wake up in the morning, ask yourself how are you doing? If you can respectfully answer that question to the fullest then I know that you must be doing alright. The next time you walk up to someone, I want you to think about your life and how you can help them be a better person. We were all put on this earth to be servants. We are to be servants of one another. When I think of servants, I think of Ms. Rosetta Jones. She is the epitome of a superwoman. She is someone I met along the way and has been an inspiration in my life. She will help you with anything you may be going through. What I like about her is that she truly cares about people. You can feel it. She makes you feel like you belong. We need more people in the world like her. Ms. Rosetta Jones, you are a G.O.A.T., (The Greatest Of All Time)! You keep doing what you're doing because people need you. I need you to be who you are.

Ms. Rose. Hey mama! I'm so glad that I met you. You have been a wonderful person inside and out. I truly do certain things just because you have inspired it. You correct me, enlighten me, you agree with me, you disagree with me. We have had some of the most interesting conversations ever. You are someone that everyone needs to have in their life. If you don't have a Ms. Rose then you are missing out.

Ms. Phillips has been a great addition to my life and I can't thank her enough for all of her guidance and kindness. You are truly a renaissance woman.

Ms. Wright. You should have a chapter all by yourself. You continue to uplift and encourage me on a daily basis. You have been my rock and my anchor for a long time. I give God praise for you.

Ms. Cooper. You know I love you. You are everybody's grandma. I'm not saying that you are old, but you are smart as a whip. I love you just for being who you are. You have counseled many and you have always supported me.

Ms. C Harris. What can I say? You have been a friend for a long time. I cherish our friendship and I pray that God blesses your life in abundance because you have blessed others with your wisdom. May God bless you and be good to you for you deserve it.

Ms. K Harris and Mr. E Harris. I love you. You all have done a lot for me and I thank you. I honestly would NOT have been able to produce one of my plays "Grandma's House" without you all. Ms. K your acting is superb. You are one of my favorite theatrical actresses. I've learned a lot about theatre through our friendship. I'm glad I met you. I'm glad God let us cross paths. It was all in his plan. You are a jewel. Just precious.

Mrs. Wicker you are a great spirit. You taught me to always capitalize the Lord's name. Lol. You are a bold woman of God and you have a heart like none other. Teach us how to be kind because you exemplify that perfectly. The World is waiting on your book.

Ms. Tuwanna you are a songbird for our generation. I'm glad to say that I promote you. Your angelic voice is powerful. I'm glad that you are using your voice for the Kingdom. You are a friend til the end.

Ms. Markie you have always assisted and supported me with every event. You have the skills to coordinate events with ease. You are truly walking in your calling. Love you and glad to call you friend.

Ms. Langford I love that you have been willing to help me and impart financial wisdom.

You are so kind and you only want the best. Everyone needs someone like you. I do certain things today just because you taught me to. You are a bold woman of God with the heart of an angel.

Pastor Allen you have inspired me in all things related to ministry. You have given me platforms that I am still grateful for today. You have given me so much and I can only say thank you. May God bless you. You will NOT BE denied of God's favor for your life.

Ms. Marissa words can't express. You are the best assistant one can ask. More than an assistant but you are a friend. I love you for simply being you. We have seen a lot of things together and I thank you for many years to come. Hang in there with me.

Aunt Lois I love you for God has shined his light on your life. Your house is the cleanest one I know. You are a virtuous woman. Thank you for being what God has called you to be.

Aunt Edna you have been a firm rock. You have wisdom beyond this world. God knew exactly what he was doing when he created you. Your words of wisdom have been imparted in my life and I will keep them from years to come.

As I close the chapter I want to thank each of you for reading about my life. My prayer is that you love each other and keep each other lifted. God has given each of us a talent. What is yours?

Find your talent, find your gift. God is whatever you need him to be. Don't live your life but live your life based according to God's unchanging word. For it is sweet.

Ask yourself "How are you doing"? And don't answer until you are sure.

I'm Seriously Joking...LOL

I'm FINE and YOU???

Stay Connected

I'd love to hear from you.

Share your thoughts on the book.

Facebook: Johnnie Busch

Email me:

Johnniebuschjr1@yahoo.com

Call us 770-780-9640 (Ask for Marissa)

Made in the USA
Columbia, SC
06 September 2022

65874729R00074